THE TRESTLE
AT POPE
LICK CREEK

Naomi Wallace

BROADWAY PLAY PUBLISHING INC
224 E 62nd St, NY NY 10065-8201
212 772-8334 fax: 212 772-8358
BroadwayPlayPub.com

THE TRESTLE AT POPE LICK CREEK
© copyright 2000 by Naomi Wallace

First printing: June 2000
This printing: March 2014
I S B N: 978-0-88145-180-1

Book design: Marie Donovan
Typeface: Palatino
Copy editing: Michele Travis
Printed and bound in the U S A

THE TRESTLE AT POPE LICK CREEK was first
produced on 14 March 1998 at the Actors Theater
of Louisville as part of the Humana Festival of New
American Plays (Jon Jory, Artistic Director; Sandy
Speer, Managing Director) The cast and creative
contributors were:

PACE ....Tami Dixon
DALTON... Michael Linstroth
GIN...Marion Mccorry
DRAY..Michael Medeiros
CHAS...Jonathan Bolt

Director.. Adrian Hall
Scenic design.. Paul Owen
Costume design.. Jeanette deJong
Lighting design .... Greg Sullivan
Sound design...................................... Martin R Desjardins
Properties design...................................... Ron Riall
Fight director ....Steve Rankin
Stage manager..Paul Mills Holmes
Assistant stage manager .... Kathy Preher
Dramaturg .... Michael Bigelow Dixon
Casting.. Laura Richin Casting

THE TRESTLE AT POPE LICK CREEK was first produced in New York on 11 June 1999 at the New York Theater Workshop (James C Nicola, Artistic Director; Jo Beddoe, Managing Director). The cast and creative contributors were:

PACE .... Alicia Goranson
DALTON .... Michael Pitt
GIN .... Nancy Robinette
DRAY .... David Chandler
CHAS .... Philip Goodwin

Director .... Lisa Peterson
Scenic design .... Riccardo Hernandez
Costume design .... Katherine Roth
Lighting design .... Scott Zielinski
Original music & sound design .... David Van Tieghem
Fight director .... Rick Sordelet
Dialect consultant .... Sarah Felder
Production stage manager .... Martha Donaldson
Assistant stage manager .... Katie J Garton

CHARACTERS & SETTING

PACE CREAGAN, *a girl, seventeen years old*
DALTON CHANCE, *a boy, fifteen years old*
GIN CHANCE, DALTON'*s mother, forty one years old*
DRAY CHANCE, DALTON'*s father, a few years* GIN'*s senior*
CHAS WEAVER, *a jailer, Brett's father, early fifties*

Time: 1936

Place: A town outside a city. Somewhere in the United States.

Note: Accents of the characters should be as "neutral" as possible, an accent from "somewhere" in the U S. Characters touch each other only when indicated in the script.

Set: should be minimal and not "realistic".

Nothing in the world is single.
Percy Bysshe Shelley

to Howard Zinn,
dear friend and teacher.
And to my childhood friends in Kentucky,
who let me in

ACT ONE

Prologue

(Darkness. Then we see DALTON *sitting upstage, in a corner. His back is all we see. Beside him is a small candle. From the light of the candle,* DALTON *makes hand shadows. We can see the shadows but we cannot discern what they are.)*

DALTON: This is a. Horse. *(He makes another hand shadow.).* This is a swan. No. Not a swan, shit. A falcon. Yeah. A falcon. No. There's no claw. It's a duck. *(He makes another hand shadow.)* Now it's a turtle. There's the shell. But hell. It could be a fish. With a fin.

(He makes another hand shadow. PACE *appears. She is there but not there. Standing behind* DALTON*)*

PACE: That's not a fish, Dalton Chance. You should know better. That's a bird. A pigeon. The kind that live under the trestle.

*(*DALTON *slowly turns and peers into the darkness. He doesn't see* PACE*, though she is visible to us. He calls softly.)*

DALTON: Creagan? Pace Creagan? Is that you? *(He stands up. He yells at her.)* You go to hell Pace Creagan!

*(*PACE *tips the candle over and there is darkness.)*

(End Prologue)

Scene One

(Months earlier, two youths, PACE *and* DALTON, *run to meet under the trestle at Pope Lick Creek.* PACE *gets there ahead of* DALTON. *They are both out of breath.)*

DALTON: You had a head start!

PACE: Nah. You haven't got any lungs in that puny chest of yours. Listen to you rattle.

DALTON: I'm not rattlin'.

PACE: Yeah you are. What've you got in there? A handful of nails.

DALTON: Twisted my ankle.

PACE: Yeah, yeah.

DALTON: So this is it, huh?

*(*DALTON *and* PACE *look up above them.)*

PACE: Yep.

DALTON: It's not that high up.

PACE: Almost a hundred feet. From the creek up.

DALTON: Some creek. There's no water: it's dry.

PACE: Don't care; can't swim anyway. What time is it?

DALTON: Coming up to seven.

PACE: Exact time.

DALTON: *(Guessing)* Six forty-one.

PACE: She comes through at seven ten. Sometimes seven twelve. Sometimes she'll come on at seven nine for ten days straight and then bang, she's off three minutes. She's never exact; you can't trust her. That's what I like.

DALTON: How many times have you done it?

PACE: Twice. Once with Jeff Farley. Once alone.

DALTON: You're lyin'. Jeff Farley never ran it.

PACE: Nope. Never did. Tied his shoes on real tight, took two deep breaths, said "I'm ready when you are". And then he heard that whistle. Aren't a lot of people can hear that whistle.

DALTON: So you didn't do it twice.

PACE: I would of but he turned tail and ran.

DALTON: So how many times then? Just once?

PACE: Once. And that's once more than you.

DALTON: Yeah. Who was witness?

PACE: No one here to see me.

DALTON: You're lying.

PACE: Whatever you say.

DALTON: Did you run it or not?

PACE: Sure. Once.

DALTON: How come I don't believe you?

PACE: Me and you, we'll have witnesses. Philip, Lester and Laura Sutton will be here at seven-o-five.

DALTON: No. No way. You said just you and me as witness.

PACE: If you get scared and run, who's to say you won't lie and say I chickened too?

DALTON: You said just you and me.

PACE: It'll be just you and me. Up there. Down here in the creek bed we'll have the three stooges watching us. Keeping tabs. Taking notes. And you can be sure they'll check our pants when we're done and see who's shit.

DALTON: You know. You don't talk like a girl. Should.

PACE: *(Meaning it)* Thanks.

DALTON: But you look like one. So I guess you are.

PACE: Want me to prove it?

DALTON: No.

PACE: How old are you?

DALTON: Sixteen. In a couple of months.

PACE: *(Nears him)*. Well, well. Almost a man. *(Pushes him backwards, but not too hard)* Listen to me, Dalton Chance, two years my junior, and shut up. Here's what we're going to do.

DALTON: Just spell it out for me. Once and clear.

PACE: Okay. She's pulling eight cars at seventy tons apiece at eighty five. Not a big one, as far as they go. But big enough. The engine herself's one hundred and fifty three tons. And not cotton, kid. Just cold, lip smackin' steel. Imagine a kiss like that. Just imagine it.

DALTON: How do you know what the train weighs?

PACE: I looked her up. The year, the weight, the speed.

DALTON: So you can read.

PACE: Yeah, well. You and her are coming from opposite sides, right? You've got to time it exact 'cause you need to make it across before she hits the trestle. It's like playin' chicken with a car, only she's bigger and you're not a car. The kick is once you get half way across, don't turn back and try to out-run her. You lose time like that. Just face her and go.

DALTON: So what if you know it's too close? You go for the side, right?

PACE: There's no side.

DALTON: Yes there is.

PACE: There's no side. Look at it.

DALTON: There's a side.

PACE: What's the matter with you? Look at the tracks. Look at them. There are no sides.

DALTON: So what do you do if you can't make it across before she starts over?

PACE: You make the cross. That's all there is to it.

DALTON: But what if you can't?

PACE: Remember Brett Weaver?

DALTON: That's different. He was drunk.

PACE: He was not.

DALTON: Yes he was. He was drunk.

PACE: Say that again and I'll punch you.

DALTON: The papers said he was drunk.

PACE: Brett wasn't drunk. He was just slow.

DALTON: Slow? He was on the track team.

PACE: That night he was slow.

DALTON: How do you know?

PACE: I just know.

DALTON: Well. I've had a look like I told you I would and I've decided: I'm not crossing.

PACE: I knew it. I knew it.

DALTON: Only a drunk or an idiot'd play that game. Not me.

PACE: You got the heart of a rabbit. A dead rabbit. And now you owe me a buck.

DALTON: No way. I never said for certain. I said maybe. And you said it was safe. You didn't say anything about there being no safety sides. You said it was a piece of cake.

PACE: It is a piece of cake. If you time it right.

DALTON: Forget it.

PACE: You're breaking the deal. Pay me a buck right now or else.

DALTON: I said no.

PACE: *(Calmly pulls a switch blade)* Then I'll hurt you.

DALTON: Put that away. You're warped. That's what everyone says at school: Pace Creagan is warped.

PACE: Then why'd you come up here with me? I'm not even your friend.

DALTON: No. You're not my friend. My friends don't pull knives.

PACE: You were starting to like me, though. I could tell. You said you'd run it with me.

DALTON: I said I might. I thought it could be fun. Warped people can be fun sometimes.

PACE: If you back down everyone will know.

DALTON: I don't care. I don't have a fan club.

PACE: Mary Ellen Berry is coming as witness too.

DALTON: No she's not.

PACE: I asked her to. And she knows you've got a fancy for her.

DALTON: Big deal. I asked her out. She turned me down. End of story.

PACE: She says you're too short.

DALTON: I'm not short.

PACE: I don't think she was talking height.

DALTON: I'm leaving.

PACE: Hey. I told her to give you a chance. She likes me. She listens to me. I told her you were going to cross the trestle with me. She said "oh". You know, like she was thinking things.

DALTON: What things?

PACE: You know. The way girls think things. One, two, three, about face. Change of season. Oh. She said "oh" like she was about to change her mind.

DALTON: Mary Ellen's popular. Why would she listen to you?

PACE: *(Shrugs)* I once told her to take off her clothes and she did.

DALTON: And what does that mean?

PACE: It means I can run faster than she can so she does what I tell her to do. And she'll be here tonight. She's coming to watch us cross.

DALTON: You had a look at her? Naked? What's she like?

PACE: I'd say she's on the menu. Front, back, and in reverse. You'd like her.

DALTON: How would you know what I like? You're not good looking.

PACE: Yeah. But that's got nothing to do with trains.

DALTON: So how close were you that time you crossed?

PACE: I'd say I had 'bout eight seconds leeway.

DALTON: Eight seconds. Sure.

PACE: A kid could do it. Look. We won't do it tonight, okay. We'll work up to it. Tonight we'll just watch her pass. Take her measure. Check her steam. Make sure we got it down. Then when we're ready, we'll run her. It'll be a snap.

DALTON: A snap. What if you trip?

PACE: Brett tripped.

DALTON: He was messed up. Even if he wasn't drunk. He used to hit himself in the face just for the fun of it. Brett was mental. He'd hit his own nose until it bled.

PACE: Brett wasn't mental.

DALTON: I saw Brett hit himself. I saw him do it.

PACE: It's none of your business.

DALTON: You were his girl.

PACE: We were friends. I never kissed him. And you're gonna run the trestle. One of these days.

DALTON: How come?

PACE: 'Cause if you don't your life will turn out just like you think it will: quick, dirty and cold.

DALTON: Hey. I might go to college when I graduate.

PACE: You're not going to college. None of us are going to college.

DALTON: I got the grades for it. That's what Mr Pearson says.

PACE: And who's gonna pay for it? Look at your shoes.

DALTON: Huh?

PACE: Your shoes. If your Mom's putting you in shoes like that then you aren't going to college. *(Beat)* Come on. Let's go up and watch.

DALTON: If I can't go to college, I'll just leave.

PACE: Some things should stay in one place, Dalton Chance. You're probably one of them.

(End Scene One)

Scene Two

(DALTON, *some months later, in an empty cell. He looks
older now, dishevelled. He just stares. And stares. At
nothing. After some moments* CHAS, *the jailer, enters.
He seems friendly enough.* DALTON *doesn't acknowledge*
CHAS's *presence.* CHAS *slips from one subject to the next,
with hardly a pause.)*

CHAS: On break. Thought I'd sit it out with you. The
other guy, across the hall. He's looking for grass in
his cell. Thinks he's a moose. Could be some other
herbivore but every now and then he lets out this call
and it sounds close enough to a moose. Yesterday, a
bug. Some kind of a beetle, I think, with huge claws.
He used his arms like pinchers. Opening and closing
them. Opening and closing. For hours. Wayne was
leaning in to give him some grub and the next minute
he caught Wayne around the neck. Almost choked him
to death. While I was prying him off he's making this
sound. A beetle sound, I guess. Sort of like... *(He makes
a "beetle sound".)* Self respect: gone. Was the manager
of the Plate Glass Company. A real Roosevelt man.
Good to his men, though he laid them off. Then his
head went pop one day and he started breaking up
the plant. Glass everywhere. Wrecked half the place.
Even the W P A says close it down. No one needs glass
these days. Might want glass but they don't need it.
Mister Roosevelt, I say, want to buy some glass? Them
up high's got the money to want. They don't have to
go by need. What kind of a beetle was it, you think?
Big pinchers. Opening and closing. How'd the visit
go? I know your folks. Nice people. Sorry to hear your
Daddy's still out of work. But who isn't? Well, I'm not.
I'm still here. Could be somewheres else, like Spain
shooting some whatyoucallem, but I might get killed
and then bein' here looks better. I had a boy like you.
You must have known my Brett at school. Big fellow.

Fast runner? Moose's easier to identify. Distinctive. My break's about up. So what do you think, kid? How many years do you think you'll get? Or will they hang you? When they hang you the last thing you hear is your own neck break. And if you got a thick neck bone, a strong one, a young one, then it takes a while to break clean through, sometimes hours, and all the while you're dying you're hearing it snappin' and crackling and poppin', just like a stick on the fire. So what do you think?

(CHAS *gets no response so he shrugs and leaves the cell.*)

DALTON: A stag beetle. That's what kind it was.

(End Scene Two)

Scene Three

(DALTON *is trying to get the shoes off his mother's feet after she's come home from work.*)

DALTON: Yeah it does. I read it at the drugstore.

GIN: Just leave it.

DALTON: All your nerves're squashed up in the ball of your foot. Stop wiggling.

(DALTON *gets one of her shoes off. She relaxes now as he massages her feet.*)

GIN: How's the math going at school?

DALTON: *(Teasing)* You've got seven toes.

GIN: Woman on the right of me, Barbara Hill, laid off Tuesday. Woman on my left, laid off today. Just waiting my turn.

DALTON: You've been there forever. They need you.

GIN: How is he?

DALTON: Quiet.

GIN: Yeah, quiet.

(GIN *unwraps a small stack of plates. Looks at them. Then wraps them up again*)

GIN: It's getting harder to find the plates. Even the Salvation is running short. I don't want to use the ones my mother gave me. Might have to one of these days.

DALTON: It'll be okay.

(DALTON *is finished with* GIN's *feet. He begins to unpin her hair and then brush it. She lets him.*)

GIN: You got anything better to do with your afternoons than take care of an old mother when she comes home from work? You should be out with the boys. Yelling. Falling down. Doing fun things boys do. What do boys do for fun?

DALTON: You know the trestle up at Pope Lick? Well, I was with a girl there this afternoon, after school.

GIN: Hmmm.

DALTON: Name's Pace Creagan. We watched the train come through.

GIN: Boy got killed up there a couple of years ago.

DALTON: It's not a big train but it's big up close. And loud.

GIN: You kiss her?

DALTON: No way. She's not the kissing kind. Not pretty either.

GIN: *(Matter-of-factly)* Not that handsome yourself, Dalton.

DALTON: That's what she said.

GIN: I know the Creagans. They're all right.

DALTON: Even if I wanted to, and I'm not saying I do, I never really—you know, like how people do—kissed a girl.

GIN: Not much to it. Just open your mouth and start chewing. First time I kissed your father it was all wet and disgusting. By the second time I'd started to like him, and then it was breathing water for air, that smooth.

DALTON: I don't know.

GIN: Neither did I.

(DRAY *appears. He sits in a corner with a stool. No one speaks for some moments.* DRAY *sits with his back to them. As they speak* DALTON *walks over and lights* DRAY's *candle, casually; he does this all the time for his father.*)

DALTON: I need some new shoes.

GIN: I know that.

DALTON: I'll get a job.

GIN: You've got school.

(DRAY *makes a hand shadow on the wall.*)

GIN: And no one's hiring.

DALTON: You know, the train that comes through Pope Lick, the engine weighs one hundred and fifty three tons. That's what Pace says.

(DRAY *makes another.* DALTON *watches his father. He moves to put his hand on his father's shoulder but his father looks at him, like a warning, so* DALTON *withdraws his hand.*)

GIN: Trains. Yeah. Huge, sweatin', steamin', oil spittin' promises when I was a girl. Always taking someone away, never bringing someone back. I couldn't get used to it.

DALTON: I'm going out. *(He kisses his mother on the cheek, then moves away.)* When you were fifteen. Like me, Mother. What did you want?

(DRAY makes another hand shadow.)

GIN: Someone to look me straight in the face and tell me flat out that I wasn't going anywhere.

DALTON: Yeah? Well then say it to me. Go on. Say it to me.

GIN: *(Quietly)* Dalton.

DALTON: Say: Dalton, my boy. You're not going anywhere.

(GIN is silent, then:)

GIN: You're my child.

DALTON: *(Quietly)* That doesn't make any difference.

(DALTON exits. DRAY stops making hand shadows. He is still.)

GIN: *(She just looks at DRAY's back.)* Touch me.

(DRAY is still. He turns to look at her, then slowly looks away.)

(End Scene Three)

Scene Four

(PACE and DALTON at the trestle, a few days later)

PACE: We need to watch her for days and days. Studyin'. Studyin'. And then one night we'll run her.

DALTON: Sure. One night.

PACE: There's a simple reason we're biding our time. Waiting for the moment that counts: We don't want to die. Now repeat after me: We don't want to die.

DALTON: We don't want to die.

PACE: So we'll be patient.

DALTON: Yeah. Until Christmas. I'll be getting some new shoes. And then I'll hook a job. Move up.

PACE: That's against the laws of gravity. Besides, you can't move up when you've got no teeth.

DALTON: I've got teeth.

PACE: You won't in a few years.

DALTON: You've got no determination. No plan for the future.

PACE: Yeah, but I watch.

DALTON: Watch what?

PACE: Things. People. I've been watching. Tomorrow. Today. For years. And this is how things are. You and me and the rest of us kids out here, we're just like. Okay. Like potatoes left in a box. You ever seen a potato that's been left in a box? The potato thinks the dark is the dirt and it starts to grow roots so it can survive, but the dark isn't the dirt and all it ends up sucking on is a fistful of air. And then it dies.

DALTON: I'm not a potato.

PACE: Yes you are.

DALTON: No I'm not. Potatoes can't run. I can. And when we decide to do it, I'm gonna make it over that trestle before you're half way across. Until then, I'm going home.

PACE: What time is it?

DALTON: Six fifty one.

PACE: Tell you what. We'll have a practice first.

DALTON: What kind of practice?

PACE: A real kind. Almost. Just to warm up. Pop the bones. Roll the blood over. You know.

(PACE *opens the paper bag she has with her. In it are a pair of boy's pants. She starts to take off her dress, not caring a bit that* DALTON *is there.*)

DALTON: Jesus.

PACE: Would you practice running the trestle in a dress?

(DALTON *turns away.*)

PACE: You can look if you want.

DALTON: No thanks. You're not my type.

(PACE *continues changing.*)

PACE: *(Casually)* Why not?

DALTON: You're loud. You're hands are dirty. You stare. *(Beat)* And you're not pretty, really.

PACE: You said that before.

DALTON: Well, it keeps coming back to me.

PACE: Anything else, kid?

DALTON: There'll be more once I get to know you.

PACE: I'm ready.

(DALTON *turns around.* PACE *is dressed in pants and a shirt, perhaps her brother's. She throws the dress at* DALTON.)

PACE: Smell it.

DALTON: No way.

PACE: Baby.

(DALTON *smells the dress.*)

PACE: Well?

DALTON: It smells nice. Flowery. Like a girl.

PACE: *(Cuffs him as she snatches the dress back)* Want to know what I don't like about you, Dalton Chance? You're a good boy. A very good boy.

DALTON: So what's that mean?

PACE: It means someone, before it's too late, has got to break you in half. *(Sighs)* I guess it'll have to be me.

(End Scene Four)

Scene Five

(The present. DALTON *in his cell, turned away from* CHAS*)*

CHAS: Now him over there, he doesn't know who his mother is. A turtle doesn't consider those things. Want to know how I know he's a turtle? *(He demonstrates, impressively, a turtle, moving its neck in and out of its shell.)* I know what you're thinking: could be a goose. I thought of that. But a goose doesn't do this— *(He moves his head slowly from side to side, then cocks his head to one side, opens his mouth and eats.)* A goose doesn't eat like a turtle. How you feelin, boy? What're you thinking? Still won't talk. Still won't talk. But they got it on record when they brought you in: Yeah, I killed her. That's what you said. Why didn't you lie? They don't have a witness. Four words. Just four words: Yeah, I killed her. But won't say why. Won't say how. What kind of a game are you playing? Well, they'll find it out. They know about kids. I had a boy your age. Couple of years older than you. Not much to him. But he was my son. *(Beat)* To think. He was just a kid like you. Scared of nothing. Yeah. Scared of nothing cause you are nothing. Half of you kids wanting to kill, the rest wanting to die. Ordering death like it's a nice, cold drink and you're going to suck it down in one gulp and then get up and walk away from it. Right. Kids. Just want to eat, fuck and tear the ornaments off the tree. But only if you don't have to get out of bed in the morning to do it. The whole damn country's going to hell cause of your kind. *(Beat)* You should have

killed your own self instead. That's what they say.
(Beat) I loved my boy Brett. But I never could figure
what he was. Something kinda small. Like a wheel,
maybe. Something that spins in place in the dark. He
had a gap in his heart. He was empty. I know; I was
his father. Sometimes he'd ask me to embrace him.
(Shrugs) He was my son. *(Beat)* So he'd be here, in my
arms, sniffling like a baby. But there was nothing. I
was holding him. He was in my arms. But it was like
holding onto. Nothing. *(Beat)* What's it feel like to be
like that? Huh? What's it feel like to be that empty?
(Begins to take off his shirt) I'm going to have to hate
you, I guess. There's not much choice.

(CHAS *stands over* DALTON. DALTON *is shivering and does
not respond.* CHAS *puts his shirt around* DALTON.)

CHAS: I'll bring you some dinner. You've lost weight.
Hard not to do in here.

(End Scene Five)

Scene Six

(DALTON, GIN *and* PACE *sitting together. There is a
strained feeling.* DALTON *wants things to be nice.)*

GIN: Dalton made a clock for his science project. Didn't
you, Dalton?

DALTON: That was last year. This year I made a scale.
To measure things on.

GIN: A scale. That's right. I use it in the kitchen. To
measure flour. It works real well. You want to try it,
Pace?

PACE: I don't do much with flour.

GIN: Oh. *(Beat)* But I'm sure you help your mother in
the kitchen.

(DALTON *speaks before* PACE *can answer.*)

DALTON: Pace likes to sew. Don't you?

(PACE *just looks at* DALTON.)

DALTON: She makes her own clothes. Tell her you make your own clothes, Pace.

PACE: I make my own clothes. My mother's not what she used to be.

GIN: That's nice. I mean, about your clothes. What did your mother used to be?

PACE: Hopeful. *(Beat)* Thank you for the tea, Mrs Chance. It was very sweet.

GIN: That's how we like it here. In our home.

(*They all sit in an awkward silence. After some moments,* PACE *places the large bag she's brought on the table.*)

DALTON: Pace said she brought something for you, mother.

GIN: My, that's nice. You didn't need to, really.

PACE: I made it in science class. Like Dalton did.

(PACE *unwraps the bag to reveal a strange mechanical engine. It looks impressive.*)

GIN: Oh. That's. Nice. What is it?

PACE: It's a beam engine.

GIN: I see...

PACE: The beam engine was the first practical working steam engine. It's simple: fire here at the bottom heats the water, the steam forces up the piston and it's cooled, fast, by spraying cold water on the cylinder. This turns the steam back to water and makes a vacuum in the space under the piston.

GIN: Piston.

DALTON: It's a present, Mother.

PACE: You see, the pressure of air outside the cylinder then pushes the piston back down again. And so on. The crosspiece joining the engine to the pump gives it its name: "beam" engine.

GIN: This is a train you've got here?

PACE: An engine. But it's an older model.

GIN: Looks kind of small to me.

PACE: The original was bigger than both of us.

GIN: Well, start it up then.

PACE: Doesn't work. Did once. Second time, my father he was leaning over it to have a look, caught his beard on fire. Third time: bang. Not a big one but I got a piece of glass in my arm.

GIN: Sounds unpredictable.

PACE: It's the only thing I had of my own to give you. *(Beat)* I didn't get a good grade on it.

GIN: You're two years older than Dalton.

DALTON: Mother.

PACE: Almost.

GIN: He's been seeing a lot of you these past weeks.

DALTON: Can we have some more tea?

PACE: You ever hear of Cugnot, Mrs Chance? Nicholas Cugnot. Made the first steam machine that moved. Crawled two miles-per-hour before it blew up. That was in France. 1769, I think. The government put Cugnot in prison. Explosion didn't hurt anyone. Never understood why they put him in jail.

GIN: My son doesn't know a thing about trains.

PACE: I think they were afraid. Not of the machine, but of Cugnot. They'd never seen anything like that moved by steam. Just plain old water *(Makes the sound of steam)*

into steam. It must have shaken them up somehow.
Just to see it. They couldn't forgive him.

GIN: What do you want with Dalton?

DALTON: Christ. We're just having tea.

GIN: Hush up.

(DALTON *shuts up.*)

GIN: We're a family here, Pace. A regular family. My
husband, Dalton and me. Lots of trouble out there, lots
of bad weather. But we take care of each other; nothing
out there we need. I want you to know that.

PACE: You know the Union Pacific? They're gonna
build the biggest steam locomotives in the world. The
engine and tender'll weigh over five hundred tons.
Colossal. They'll be 4-8-8-4 articulated locomotives
with two sets of driving wheels, each with their own
cylinders.

(GIN *just stares at* PACE.)

PACE: I'm sorry, Mrs Chance. But me and Dalton. It's
none of your business.

GIN: Cylinders, huh? Driving wheels. Articulated
locomotives. If you're thinking to trick my son—

DALTON: I can't believe this...

PACE: Mrs Chance, I'm not sweet on your son's
locomotive system, if that's what you mean. We've
never touched each other. I've got nothing to be
ashamed of. Though I did tell him to take off his
clothes once, under the trestle.

GIN: To take off his—

DALTON: Pace!

PACE: Shut up, Dalton. (*Beat*) And then once on the
tracks. A hundred feet up. Wasn't a train in sight. It
was kinda chilly that evening, but it was safe.

GIN: I think you better leave now.

PACE: He doesn't like me, really. He says I'm loud.

GIN: *(To* DALTON*)* You took off your clothes?

PACE: He's your son. He does what he's told.

GIN: Why would you do such a thing? Anyone might have seen you.

PACE: Yeah. I did. And he's not like an engine at all. Nah. Dalton's pale. Real pale. No steam. How's he keep warm? Doesn't know the first thing about cylinders. And he's so light, what keeps him where he stands? On the tracks, slip, slip, slip. No traction. Now, the Big Boys, the new ones, they'll need near ten tons of coal per hour in their firebox. And the grate where the coal'll be burned is bigger than a kitchen.

*(*GIN *just stares at* PACE.*)*

PACE: Imagine it. That's what we're coming to.

(End Scene Six)

Scene Seven

*(*DALTON *and* PACE *at the trestle)*

PACE: Let's start here. On this tie.

DALTON: What tie? The tracks up there.

PACE: Imagine it, stupid.

DALTON: Right.

PACE: See, this tie's marked with a red X.

DALTON: Maybe I want to start on this other tie.

PACE: Look. It's tradition, Okay. Besides, Brett made this X so let's use it. Now, you crouch down like this. Go on. Yeah. That's right. Like at a track meet. Point your skinny rear to the stars. Got it.

DALTON: I'll count down.

PACE: Now when you say "Go" we run like crazy to the other side. But don't check your feet. You'll trip if you check your feet. Just trust that your feet know where to go.

DALTON: I hear you.

PACE: You're playin' chicken with the train so you keep your eyes on the engine headed towards you. It'll look like she's real close but she won't be. If you start when I tell you to, you'll have enough time to make it across and have dinner before she starts over the trestle. Ready?

DALTON: Pace?

PACE: Yeah?

DALTON: My legs are shaking.

PACE: This is practice, Dalton. There's no train down here.

DALTON: My legs aren't so sure.

PACE: On the count of three. Come on.

DALTON & PACE: One, two, three—

DALTON: Wait! *(He seems to be looking over an edge.)*

PACE: Don't look. You'll lose your nerve.

DALTON: It's a long way down.

PACE: Why don't we just walk it. Give me your hand. *(She takes his hand and begins to walk him)*

DALTON: God we're high up.

PACE: *(Smacks him)* Keep your eyes on the other side. Pretend that we're running.

(DALTON and PACE pretend they're running, and run in place.)

DALTON: We are. I'm out of breath.

PACE: We're almost there. Yeah. Yeah. Grease those knees. And now you trip.

DALTON: What?

PACE: You trip.

(PACE *trips him so he falls to the ground*)

DALTON: Hey! What the— You tripped me. Hey—

PACE: It might happen.

DALTON: Why'd you—

(DALTON *tries to get up. She knocks him back down, hard.*)

PACE: You might trip. Anything's possible. We got to be ready for it.

DALTON: But I wouldn't've tripped! You pushed me!

PACE: Don't get up. Just sit there. Like you tripped. Let's say I'm flaggin' behind and you look over your shoulder to see how I'm doing and you trip. And just as you trip you hear her coming around the hill. (*She makes the sound of a train whistle.*)

DALTON: You sound like a kitten. It's like this. (*He makes an even better whistle.*)

PACE: Yeah! And you can hear her cold slathering black hell of a heart barrelling towards the trestle and it sounds like this:

(*Together they make an engine sound, surprisingly well.*)

PACE: But you've twisted your ankle.

DALTON: Yeah. And I can hardly stand. It feels like my foot's coming off. (*Makes a painful gasp*) I try to run but I can only hobble. And the train, she's just about to cross.

PACE: And then there I am. At your side.

DALTON: No. I'd slow you down and you know it. You just pass me by. *(Makes the sound of an arrow flying)* Like an arrow. You've got to save your own skin.

PACE: Yeah, but I can't just leave you there.

DALTON: Yes you can.

PACE: You'll be killed.

DALTON: I'll be torn apart.

PACE: So I put my arm around your waist and start to drag you down the tracks with me. It's hard going. We've only got fifty feet or so 'til we're clear.

DALTON: But the train. *(He lets out the terrible scream of a whistle.)* So you drop me.

PACE: No.

DALTON: You drop me and run. You run for your life.

PACE: No. I don't leave you. I—

DALTON: You make it across. Just in time. Alone.

PACE: I drag you with me.

DALTON: And as you clear the tracks, you feel the hurtling wind of her as she rushes by you, so close it's like she's kissing the back of your neck, so close she pulls the shirt right up off you without popping the buttons. *(Beat)* And then? And then you hear me scream.

(DALTON lets out a terrible scream and at the same time PACE screams:)

PACE: I save you!

(They are silent some moments.)

DALTON: And then? And then nothing. The train, she disappears over the trestle and on down the track. *(Beat)* You, Pace Creagan, are standing there, breathing hard—

PACE: —My heart jumping jacks, yeah, shooting dice in my chest. Snake eyes. But I'm alive. Alive!

DALTON: As for me, well, you know I'm dead. You're certain. But still you have to go back and have a look. To see what's left. Of course there's almost nothing left.

PACE: Yeah there was. There was a lot left.

DALTON: No. Just some bits of. Meat. And a running shoe. That's all. I'm mashed potatoes now. Just add some milk and stir.

PACE: He wasn't wearing running shoes.

DALTON: Hey. Take a look at my face. I'm talking to you: I'm dead.

PACE: Brett was wearing boots.

DALTON: And now maybe my Mom will be able to scrounge up some new shoes for the funeral. If she can find my feet.

PACE: *(Calmly)* Shut up. Just. Shut up. Have you ever put a shell up to your ear?

DALTON: What?

PACE: A conch shell. One of those big ones. It's not the ocean you're hearing. Or even the blood in your head. *(Makes the sound of a shell over an ear)* That's the sound. And it's been going on for years. Even now you can hear it. Listen. It's this town. Our future. You and me. *(Makes the sound again)*. Empty. No more, no less. Just. Empty.

DALTON: *(Disgusted)* I'm going home.

PACE: Wait.

DALTON: *(Leaving)* Not this time.

PACE: Take off your clothes.

DALTON: Why?

PACE: Because you want to.

(DALTON *begins to undress.* PACE *watches him. He's about to take off his underwear.*)

PACE: Stop. There. Yeah. That's enough.

(*They both watch each other.* PACE *moves closer to him, but not that close.*)

PACE: Are you cold?

DALTON: A little. (*Beat*) Well. Are you gonna touch me or what?

PACE: No. I just wanted. To look at you.

DALTON: Once you take your clothes off. Something is supposed to happen.

PACE: It already has. (*Beat*) Get dressed.

(*After a moment,* DALTON *starts to get dressed*)

(*End Scene Seven*)

Scene Eight

(DRAY *and* GIN. *He sits immobile. She uncovers a small stack of plates. She tosses one to him. Suddenly he comes alive and they are tossing a plate back and forth between them as they speak. They've done this before.*)

GIN: You've got to get out.

DRAY: I'm movin'. You just can't see it.

GIN: At the W P A office. They're helpin' people find jobs.

DRAY: A handful.

GIN: That's better than nothing.

DRAY: I don't know.

GIN: I went by the Council. They got kicked out of the church basement. Got a room in the Watson storehouse. More like a closet than a room.

DRAY: The Council. They're not government.

GIN: No, they're not. Just people out of work. Tryin' to get things going. Lots of talk about the Plate Glass factory.

DRAY: It's closed down.

GIN: Talk about opening it up again. Building it back up. Running it themselves. Machinery's still there. Most of it. It's a mess but it's all still there.

DRAY: We've got what we need. The three of us. Under this roof.

GIN: I know that.

DRAY: Sounds like you're getting involved.

GIN: No. I'm not. I'm just listening.

DRAY: My father worked there when he was a boy. There'd be explosions now and then. He wore eye wear. A lot of them didn't. Once the glass hit him in the mouth. Long thin pieces of glass. He pulled them out his cheeks with pliers, like pullin' fish bones out a fish. *(Beat)* That place doesn't belong to them, Gin. Sounds like communists.

GIN: People, Dray. Just people tired of not working. Tired of waiting for the W P A to hand out the jobs. Tired. Just tired. You know that kind of tired.

DRAY: Can't remember when I wasn't.

GIN: I remember. When you were a boy.

(DRAY almost drops a plate, but catches it. He becomes more playful.)

DRAY: You lie, Miss Ginny Carol. I was never a kid.

GIN: Yeah you were. And so was I.

DRAY: Nah. That was just a fancy idea we had about ourselves.

GIN: You didn't bring me flowers like other girls got. You brought me tomatoes.

DRAY: You can't eat flowers.

GIN: And corn. You were nineteen.

DRAY: A bucket of frogs, too. I made you close your eyes and put your hands in it. You didn't scream like most of them did. You went dead pale. I thought I might have killed you. And then you did the damnedest thing: You kissed me. Not on the cheek, either. Smack on the mouth.

GIN: I was in shock. The frogs did it to me. *(Beat)* You hardly kissed me back.

DRAY: I was in shock. Never had a girl put her tongue in my mouth before. We weren't even engaged. You took me to the storm shelter and took off your dress. You pushed me to my knees. I never kissed a girl there before. I never even thought it could be done. You went dead pale. That was the second time I thought I killed you. When you finally let me get to my feet, you had a clump of my hair in each of your hands, you'd pulled on my head so hard.

GIN: I wasn't tired back then. And neither were you.

DRAY: No, I guess I wasn't. *(Beat)* There were two things I wanted when I was a boy: one was to land a good job at the foundry, the other was to have you turn me into a bald man by the time I was old.

GIN: You lost quite a bit of hair over the years. Though not lately, I'm sorry to say.

(DRAY *misses a plate and it drops and breaks. Silence)*

DRAY: It was mine, Gin. Nineteen years of it.

GIN: Yeah, and what did it give you? A bad arm, a broken collar, burns across your back so deep the bath water stays in them.

DRAY: That job was mine.

GIN: We're still here.

DRAY: Yeah. And you won't ever leave me.

GIN: I won't ever leave you, Dray.

(Silence some moments)

GIN: I heard they were hiring a couple of men down at Turner's. You might—

DRAY: *(Interrupts)* I was there this morning while you were at work. They hired three men. Three men. Fifty-two of us they left standing. There wasn't a sound. For the longest time we just stood there watching the door that'd been shut. All that disappointment. Fifty-two men. Fifty-two of us. And weighin' how much? None of us eating big these days. Most of us lookin' lean. Maybe...nine thousand pounds, all of us together. That much disappointment. *(Beat)* And not a sound.

(DRAY *sits with the plate in his lap. They sit in silence some moments.* GIN *moves to touch* DRAY, *to comfort him.* DRAY *speaks gently to her.)*

DRAY: Don't touch me, Gin. I could kill you.

(End Scene Eight)

Scene Nine

(DALTON *lying asleep on the floor in a blanket. He gets up. He is shirtless. He thinks he's alone. But* GIN *is standing over him; he starts.)*

GIN: Dalton.

DALTON: You're always alone.

GIN: He hardly leaves the house.

DALTON: You'd think this might be special circumstances.

GIN: He's restless. Without you home.

DALTON: He never looked me over when I was there.

GIN: You don't have to look at someone—

DALTON: I don't need your excuses. Neither does he. From what I remember, he didn't look at you any more than he did at me.

GIN: Not long ago he used to hold me.

DALTON: Big deal. Holding someone's a cinch. You just open your arms, pop them inside, then open again and you're done. It doesn't cost. It's easy.

GIN: And the girl. What about her, then. To hold her.

(PACE *appears. While neither* GIN *nor* DALTON *sees her, sometimes they sense, at different moments, that she is "there".* PACE *is playful.*)

GIN: Was that "easy"?

DALTON: That's none of your business. *(Beat)* I don't want you here.

PACE: Was that "a cinch"?

DALTON: *(Shouts)* I didn't hold her! *(Now he is quiet.)* She held me. Pace did. But it wasn't that. Holding. Sometimes when I was with her, she wasn't there. Or when I was without her, she was there, but not there. Alone at night in bed, I could feel her breath in my ears. No.

DALTON & PACE: That's not it.

PACE: It wasn't just you and me.

DALTON: It was something more. Like at school. At school they teach you. They say it's math,

PACE: history,

DALTON: geometry, whatever. But they're teaching you to speak. Not about the world but about things. Just things: a door, a map,

PACE: a cup. Just the name of it.

DALTON: Not what a cup means, who picked it up, who drank from it,

PACE: who didn't and why;

DALTON: where a map came from, who fixed in the rivers, who'll take the wrong turn; or a door. Who cut the wood and hung it there? Why that width, that height? And who made that decision? Who agreed to it? Who didn't?

PACE: And what happened to them because of it?

DALTON: They just teach us to speak the things. So that's what we speak. But there's no past that way.

DALTON & PACE: And no future.

DALTON: Cause after you've said the thing, you move on. You don't look back. You never think to cross it, never stop and turn.

PACE: *(No longer playful)* But you stopped, didn't you, Dalton? You stopped and turned.

DALTON: She laughed at everything that seemed right.

PACE: And you didn't turn back. *(Calmly)* You son of a bitch.

(PACE retreats somewhat, but she is still "there".)

DALTON: It wasn't just at night. In the day sometimes. Not her voice but the sound of her. I could hear it. Like water running in a pipe. But that's not it. It was more like this. This cup. *(He takes his drinking cup, calmly kneels and breaks it on the floor. His hand bleeds slightly. He sorts through the pieces.)* Look. This was sand and heat. Not long ago. Other things, too. And now. It's something else. Glass. Blood. And it's broken. *(He picks up a large piece, nears* GIN.*)* I could cut you open with it.

*(*GIN *slaps* DALTON *in the face. He's taken aback, put in his place.)*

DALTON: But that's what she did to me. Cut me open and things weren't just things after that. They were more. What they'd once been and what they could be besides. I was just a kid—

PACE: —like any other. You didn't care.

DALTON: I never even thought about it. But then one day I wasn't sure. She did that to me. She made me— hesitate. In everything I did. I was. Unsure. Look. It's not a cup anymore; it's a knife.

*(*PACE *stands close to* DALTON, *but he cannot see her.)*

PACE: I could cut you open and see my face.

DALTON: And it was true. I could touch myself at night and I didn't know if it was her hand or mine. I could touch myself. I could put my hand. I could. Maybe I was asleep. I don't know but sometimes I put my hand. Inside myself.

PACE: *(Whispers to him)* And you were wet.

DALTON: I was wet. Just like a girl. It was. Yeah. Like I was touching her. Just to touch myself. *(Beat)* It wasn't right.

(Silence some moments)

GIN: Only time I ever knew things were right is when they were wrong. Everyone said your father was a mistake. After I made that one, and it worked out so well, I dedicated myself to making as many mistakes as possible in a life time. The only time I was ever sure who I was was when I was wrong. *(Beat)* I think you loved that girl.

DALTON: Yeah. Maybe that's why I killed her. Please. I want you to go.

GIN: All right.

(PACE *suddenly kicks a piece of the broken cup. It skids between* DALTON *and* GIN. GIN *looks at the broken piece. Split scene:* DRAY *is alone in another area. Perhaps up above them. In the dark. He is making awkward but somehow lovely movements about the room. Then we see he is dancing without music.*)

PACE: There's your cup, kid. Drink from it.

(*Then* DRAY *sings and dances his song.*)

DRAY: When I was still living, when I was a boy
I could sing like the water and dance like a toy.

My love she would kiss me 'til my mouth it was warmed.
There was no place on earth where we'd ever be harmed.

(*End Scene Nine*)

Scene Ten

(DALTON *and* PACE *under the trestle*)

DALTON: There's no one home at my house in the daytime. We could hang out there. Well, my Dad's at home but I'm not sure he counts as someone anymore. Ever since he got laid off at the foundry, he sits with the lights off. He's got a candle burning. Makes shadows on the wall with his hands. Spiders. Bats. You know. Rabbits.

PACE: I guess I'm supposed to think that's sad.

DALTON: You think about kissing me?

PACE: Kissing you where?

DALTON: I don't know. Here. In your yard. Or mine.

PACE: I mean where on you?

DALTON: My mouth. Where else?

PACE: Nope. We're friends.

DALTON: Like you and Brett were friends?

PACE: That was different. He was like my sister or something.

DALTON: Yeah. Yeah. Just forget it, okay. Pace Creagan isn't that kind of girl, anyhow. She pulls knives. She takes off her clothes. She pisses under the trestle.

PACE: Shits there too. I mean, why go all the way home?

DALTON: But she doesn't think about kissing.

PACE: Not on the mouth; that's common.

DALTON: Where else then?

PACE: I don't know. A place where no one else has kissed you, maybe. Everyone in the world has kissed you on the face, right?

DALTON: Keep talking.

PACE: If I ever kiss you, and I'm not saying I ever will, it will be some place even you've never thought of.

DALTON: You mean— *(He looks down at his crotch, with a sort of reserved bravado.)*

PACE: No way. You could trick me and piss on me. Look, if you want a kiss so bad, I'll give it to you, but you got to promise to take it wherever I want to plant it.

DALTON: If it's at least ten seconds long, I promise.

PACE: Agreed. Take down your pants.

DALTON: *(Suddenly afraid)* No. Wait. You said it wasn't there!

PACE: It's not. Trust me.

(With some apprehension, DALTON drops his pants.)

PACE: Turn around.

DALTON: Pace. I'm not sure—

PACE: *(Interrupts)* Shut up, kid. We got a deal.

(DALTON reluctantly turns around. PACE stands behind him, then drops to her knees.)

PACE: Count.

(PACE puts her mouth just above the back of DALTON's knee. She kisses him there and holds it.)

DALTON: One, two, three, four, five, six...seven...

(PACE slaps DALTON and he continues counting.)

DALTON: eight, nine, ten.

(PACE stands up. DALTON pulls up his pants. They look at each other.)

DALTON: Well. Yeah.

PACE: You happy now?

DALTON: Happy. Sure. *(Beat)* I'm gonna run over to my friend Sean's right now and tell him all about it. How it was great. How long it lasted. How far we went. "Sean, Sean, guess what? She tongued the back of my knee!" Is that what you did with your friend Brett? You kiss him like that too?

(PACE approaches DALTON, then spits on him and wipes her mouth.)

PACE: There. You can have it back. I wish I'd never done it.

DALTON: *(Starts to push her. He's pushing her hard backwards but she keeps her footing. The potential for violence to escalate is evident.)* Spit on me? You think you can do that? Who the hell do you think you are? Who the hell, Pace Creagan? What's so special about your kiss, huh? I could just take it, you know. I could just take it if I wanted to.

(*Now* PACE *pushes back.* DALTON *hesitates. She raises her arm to hit him but then hesitates.*)

DALTON: Go on. I'm your friend. Hit me.

PACE: I don't want to hit you. I want you to shut up. You liked it. I could tell. You're mad at me 'cause you liked it.

DALTON: I wanted you to kiss me on the mouth.

PACE: When you were counting. All the while. Couldn't you feel it? Where I was kissing you, it was on your mouth.

(DALTON *and* PACE *are quiet some moments.*)

DALTON: What I said about Brett. It was stupid.

PACE: Yeah. It was. (*Beat*) But you were wrong the other day. That's not what a train does to you. It doesn't mush you up. This train. She's a knife. That's why we loved her. Me and Brett. (*Beat*) We had a good start. Me and Brett. We both could have made it. 'Course Brett, he was faster. I expected to be running behind. But Brett was worried. About me. He was stupid like that. He turned to look over his shoulder at me and he tripped. I thought he'd just jump up and keep going so I passed him right by. We'd timed it tight, and right then that engine was so close I could smell her. (*Beat*) I thought Brett was right behind me.

DALTON: You left him on the tracks?

PACE: I thought he was running behind me. I could hear him behind me. He didn't call out. He didn't say wait up. I didn't know. Why didn't he call out?

(*There is the real sound of a whistle in the distance.*)

PACE: Not even a sound. Brett just sat there where he'd fallen. And then he stood up, slowly, like he had the time. He stood there looking at her, looking her straight in the face. Almost like it was a dare. Like: Go ahead and hit me. You can't do that to a train. You can't dare a train to hit you. Cause it will.

(Another whistle, closer this time)

DALTON: This is stupid. Brett was alone up there. No body knows.

PACE: Just stood there like she could pass right through him for all he cared. Like he wasn't going to flinch.

DALTON: Let's get out of here, it's getting late.

(He takes her arm.)

PACE: Let go of me.

DALTON: You're making this up.

PACE: Get off.

DALTON: You're out of your mind.

(DALTON tries to grab PACE again. She resists and he stumbles.)

(There is the sound of train rushing over the trestle above them. The sound is enormous. Then it disappears into the distance. DALTON has cut his hand.)

DALTON: Shit.

PACE: You all right?

DALTON: No. Cut my· hand.

PACE: Let me see.

DALTON: Just a scratch.

PACE: It's not how you think it is. The train, she doesn't mush you up. An arm here. A leg here. A shoe. No. She's cleaner than that. I walked back down the tracks after the train had passed. She cut Brett in two.

DALTON: Pace.

PACE: You know what I thought? Blocks. Two blocks, and maybe if I could fit the pieces back together again, he'd be. Whole.

DALTON: Will you shut your mouth. Please.

PACE: *(She rips a piece of cloth from her dress, bandages his hand.)* Use this. Wrap it around your hand. It'll stop the bleeding.

DALTON: Thanks. *(Beat)* You going home now?

PACE: I don't know. My Mom made a loaf for my brother's birthday tomorrow. Maybe we could weasel some out of her tonight.

DALTON: Okay.

PACE: We're going to do it for real.

DALTON: Yeah. We'll do it. We'll make the cross.

PACE: Both of us. Side by side.

DALTON: That's right.

PACE: A steady run.

DALTON: As can be.

PACE: Does your Dad really make shadow animals on the wall?

DALTON: Yep.

PACE: Can you?

DALTON: Never tried.

PACE: That's pretty neat. Not everyone can do that. I can't. *(She stands close to him, face to face for a moment.)* You won't take anything from me that I don't want to give you, Dalton. And that's a fact.

DALTON: All right. *(Beat)* Hey, I'll race you down the hill.

PACE: Nah. I'm tired. *(Beat)* Go!

(Blackout. We hear DALTON's *voice in the dark, but as though it were coming from a distance away.)*

DALTON: Hey, you—I'll catch you this time!

(End Scene Ten)

Scene Eleven

(In the semi-dark we see only the hands of someone. Two, blue hands. They move about in the dark. They "play". As though someone were hesitantly trying out their glow in the dark. Suddenly, PACE *appears, perhaps somewhere above or behind* GIN. PACE *is in the same dress we saw her wear in her earlier encounters with* DALTON. *The tear in the dress is larger. This is the only difference in her appearance. Though* PACE *is not in front of* GIN, GIN *speaks to her and looks at her as though* PACE *were right in front of her.)*

GIN: Oh. Pace.

*(*PACE *is still. She just watches* GIN.*)*

GIN: I didn't see you. I was just. Trying to get used to this. It won't come off. They're lights, almost. It doesn't hurt. Well, it hurts cause I scrub them but it does no good. This color's here to stay. One morning I go to work and I come home with blue hands. They changed chemicals again at the plant. All sixteen of us in my section got blue hands. Some of the women, they were upset when it wouldn't wash off. But we had to see it as a wonder, too. During break, we turned off the lights and standing all together, some with our arms raised, others at our side, we looked like a Christmas tree in the dark, with blue lights. Then we all put our arms over our heads like this *(Demonstrates)* and waved our fingers and we were a flock of crazy blue birds taking off. We started laughing then, and piling on top of each other, imagine it, and most of us women my age, and our hands were like blue snow balls flying this way and that. One of the girls, Victoria, she laughed so hard she peed right where she stood. Another one, Willa, she slipped in it and that had all of us roaring. *(Beat)* Then Laura Townsend said we had all better think again cause we had the hands of dead women. Well, that put an end to the fun and we went back to work. The manager said it would wear off but it won't. We even used bleach. We'll have to get used to it. Kind of ugly and kind of pretty both, isn't it? But hands aren't meant to be blue. *(Beat)* You're almost a woman yourself, Pace. Hell, I don't blame him. My husband. We're not. Close. Do you know what I mean? Like we used to be.

PACE: You asked me what I wanted with your son.

GIN: I meant no harm, girl. A mother's supposed to ask.

PACE: I was going to be different. I don't know in what way. That never mattered. But different somehow. Do you know what I mean?

GIN: There's blood on your leg.

PACE: And Dalton would be there to see it happen. That's what I was getting him ready for.

GIN: What are you doing out so late? Where's Dalton?

PACE: He'll be home. He's still out at the trestle. *(Beat)* He's not alone. He's with a girl.

GIN: Oh. Pace. I'm sorry.

PACE: I'm not. I was watching them. At first, I couldn't see them. It was dark. And there was this noise, like water rushing. Right through my head. But then I looked harder and I could see them. He stood over her. He was shaking her. But she wouldn't get up. And he was shouting. Shouting so loud. He wouldn't shut up.

GIN: Dalton wouldn't— No. Dalton's—

PACE: *(Interrupts)* But she wouldn't answer him. She hates him, I thought. And that made me glad. And then he stopped shouting. He gave up and put his head on her breast. *(Beat)* And then, well. I saw it; he kissed her. He kissed her.

GIN: There'll be other boys, Pace—

PACE: And she let him. I never let Dalton kiss me, but she did. And then, I felt him kiss her. I felt it. He was kissing her. Kissing her. But his mouth was inside of mine. And I let him. I let his mouth be inside of me like that, even though I wasn't with him anymore.

GIN: *(Moves to comfort PACE)* Come here, girl. I'm sorry.

PACE: *(Stepping backwards)* Don't touch the back of my head.

GIN: Why not?

PACE: It's gone.

(We hear a door slam loudly.)

GIN: Dalton? Dalton!

(We hear the loud slamming of the door, like a cell. The slamming echoes.)

(End Scene Eleven)

CT ONE

ACT TWO

Scene One

(It's dark in DALTON's cell but then a light appears. It's CHAS. DALTON lies sleeping on the ground. CHAS stands over DALTON, watching DALTON sleep.)

CHAS: Least you could do is turn into a boat. A little one. No oars. I could guess it. I know water.

(DALTON moans in his sleep, like a child. CHAS sings to put DALTON back to sleep.)

CHAS: Rocking on the sea, looking for my soul
Dead man's blood from an old boat hole.
Sail to the left, sail to the right,
Sail to the end in the cold moon light.
(The song ends.) Sleep of the dead. That's you. Creagan. Pace. Ring a bell? In the dead. Of night. What're you thinkin'? Are you there with her or somewhere else? *(Standing over DALTON, he begins to peel an apple. He lets the bits of peel fall across DALTON's face.)* Why do I spend my time on you, huh? Could it be I know our friend across the hall is on his way out of here? The poor man's got no wind in his jail cell. Still, he's doing this: *(He spins his head to the left and right like a weathervane.)* He's a weather vane tonight. *(Beat)* I'm waiting for you to surprise me, kid. Turn your head, open your mouth, roll your eyes, swish your feet and I'll know it: you're a fish of sorts. Could you do that? Here? Or am I wastin' time, my time, when I could be over the sea fightin'

with the Abe Lincoln, bullets and dive-bombers whistlin' and divin' and you here, sweet as baby's-breath, sleeping and moaning over a dead girl. And I'm sharing my apple. What are county jails coming to. *(Softly chants)*
Apples, apples, buy a veteran's apples,
sweet and hard as ruby rocks.
Five cents a piece, Two dollars for a box

Apples, apples, buy an old man's apples.
Fought for his country, left on his back.
Won't you taste his apples, they're black, black, black?

Whatever you are my boy, I'll find you out. I won't sleep. And little by little, you'll stop sleeping too.

(The peels falling on his face finally wake DALTON *and he screams himself awake. He sits up, not knowing where he is.)*

CHAS: Another one, kid. That's about three a night now. You're sweating 'til you stink. Hey. I got a good one. What's this:

*(*CHAS *gets down on all fours and acts out something contorted and disturbing.)*

CHAS: Come on. Make a wild guess. I'll give you a buck. And a hint: it's something you can't see, but it's there from the moment you're born 'til the moment you die. What is it?

*(*CHAS *repeats the act. This time it's more grotesque. He comes up close to* DALTON, *too close and* DALTON *backs away, frightened.)*

CHAS: Give up? *(Beat)* It's your soul.

(After some moments)

DALTON: Go to hell.

CHAS: He speaks! He speaks! And what does he tell me? Go to hell. Go to hell. That's us in here, isn't it? Just you and me, hour after hour. So tell me. Tell me.

Why'd you kill her? Think she was pregnant? Well, she
wasn't. But they say you got a chance if you say you
thought she was. Don't you want a chance, Chance?
(Beat) Why'd you kill Pace Creagan?

DALTON: Don't. Say her name.

CHAS: Pretty name. Strange. Strange girl too. Lucky
she wasn't more of a girl. More of a girl, and they'd
hang you for sure. That's what they're saying. Seen her
parents since? No. But I have. Like two grey sticks, the
man and the wife, so thin with grief they are. As they
walk, the wind blows them from one side of the road to
the other. You did that to them. You did that, boy. She
was a kid. A box of crackers. You opened her up, took
a handful and threw the rest away.

(DALTON gets to his feet.)

CHAS: That's it, boy. That's it. Let's see some life in
you. I know what's inside of you. I know what's inside.
Don't think I don't know. Here? *(He throws the small
knife down on the floor between them.)* There it is, boy.
You can use it. Go on. Show me what you really are.
What happened that night, huh? Lose your nerve? You
tried though. We know that. Dress all torn up. Head
smashed. She must have put up a hell of a fight. I bet
you liked that. That's the way you kids like it. All that
fightin' hoists your flag, gets you flappin. Got you so
edged, you couldn't hold it in. Couldn't wait. Shot
your cum all over her dress but missed the target. Oh
yeah. It was your cum all right. But Pace Creagan died
a virgin. That's what the doctor says.

*(DALTON moves away from CHAS. After some moments,
CHAS picks up the knife. He speaks gently.)*

CHAS: You want to kill me, don't you?

(DALTON shakes his head "no".)

CHAS: I can see the hate rising out the top of your head like steam. Here, take this. Go on. *(He holds out the knife.)* You got to face up to what you are. You're a killer. A kid with a shell for a heart. A head full of black water. Everything sunk. Everything drowned inside you.

(CHAS forces DALTON to hold the knife. CHAS forces the knife up to his own throat. DALTON is passive. CHAS whispers.)

CHAS: Go on. It's what makes you whole.

(CHAS laughs softly. Then suddenly DALTON shouts and forces CHAS backwards. DALTON forces CHAS to the floor with the knife to his neck.)

DALTON: I don't want to do it. You're just a man. *(It seems as though he could kill CHAS any moment.)* I can't even imagine it. Killing someone like you. With her. With Pace. I could imagine it. This what you want to hear? Okay, then. Like her parents, she was just a stick. I picked her up, carried her a little ways, and when I got tired I broke her—snap—in half. Threw the pieces to the side. Those are the facts. It was that easy. You want a reason? Okay: the only way to love someone is to kill them.

(DALTON releases CHAS. But as he moves away, CHAS suddenly grabs at his leg. DALTON attempts to shake him off, even drag him, but CHAS holds on, lying on his belly. This makes for an irritating—and almost comical— interruption for DALTON's words.)

DALTON: God damn it I did what I was told— *(Drags CHAS as he moves away)* —became what I was taught: a man with a little piece of future, 'bout as big as a dime. Only there wasn't one— Let go of my leg—There never was for most of us. That was the plan and it never was ours. But I bought that plan anyway—Get off of me— cause it was the only thing to buy. Those are the facts.

This isn't about who we are. This isn't about what we wanted.

(With effort, DALTON *breaks free.* CHAS *lies still on the floor, looking up at him.)*

DALTON: My country loves me. That's why it's killing me. It's killing my father. Those are the facts. Those are the facts of love.

(After some moments, CHAS *gets to his feet.)*

CHAS: You. You're not our children. We don't want you.

DALTON: What you were making earlier? That wasn't my soul. *(Beat)* That was yours.

(End Scene One)

Scene Two

*(*GIN *stands with her mother's blue plates behind her back.* DRAY *has cornered her.)*

DRAY: Give them to me.

GIN: Get out of this house and get your own. These were my mother's. I won't do it anymore. The Salvation was out. The woman there says to me "What're you doing with all those plates, Ma'am." I said "There's no food anymore. We eat them." I went down the road. I stopped at the dump. Next thing I'm on my hands and knees, digging through garbage to find something for you to break. That's when I started laughing. Laughed so hard two rats flew out from under me.

DRAY: Just give me one.

GIN: Not one. Not two. Not ever again.

DRAY: Gin.

GIN: Go to the jail and visit your son. Get outside. Tear the bricks from the sidewalk if you have to. I don't care.

DRAY: I can't. I'm afraid.

GIN: Of what?

DRAY: That if I go out, they won't be able to see me.

GIN: Who? Who won't be able to see you?

DRAY: People. Out walking in the road.

GIN: Yes they will.

DRAY: They'll walk right through me. (*He slowly takes off his shirt, seemingly unconsciously while he speaks.*) My mother used to tell me "Dray. You are what you do." In the Foundry, it's no rest and you've always got a burn somewhere. I never minded. I was doing. I was part of the work. Part of the day. I was. I don't know. Burning. Freezing up. Inside that buzz. Melting down alongside thirty other men. But we were there. You could see us, and we weren't just making steel, we were. I don't know. We were. Making ourselves. We were. I was. All that. Movement. Movement. And now I do. Nothing. So. Then I am. What? Yeah. Nothing.

GIN: Go talk to them. They understand. They'll listen.

DRAY: I won't have anything to do with the Council. I know what they're up to. They're gonna take something that's not theirs. They're gonna break the law.

GIN: Yeah, well sometimes you break the law or it breaks you.

DRAY: Red thoughts, Ginny.

GIN: Yeah. My thoughts are red and my hands are blue.

DRAY: *(He begins to methodically rip his shirt into pieces as he speaks. This is a violent act, but somehow he does it calmly, simply.)* They were running. Like all of us are. A few months back, up North. You know the story. *(Rips the cloth)* A strike. Out on the street. Thousands of them. Doing something about it, *(Rips the cloth)* like you say. Republic Steel brought the police out. Ten men were killed. All of them strikers. *(Rips the cloth)* Papers said the strikers started it. Weeks later. It got around. They were running away. *(Rips the cloth)* The bullets hit them in the back.

GIN: I never said I wasn't afraid.

DRAY: *(He's finished with his shirt, and is very calm.)* You can go ahead now. If you want.

GIN: Where?

DRAY: I don't know.

(GIN carefully, hesitantly touches his bare arm. DRAY closes his eyes. She touches his chest.)

DRAY: You're cold, Gin.

(She keeps touching him. Now his back)

DRAY: But it's nice. It almost burns. *(Beat)* There. That's enough.

GIN: I don't want to stop.

DRAY: I don't want to either.

GIN: I want you to kiss me.

DRAY: I can't. I might hurt you.

GIN: I don't care.

DRAY: *(Gently)* Get away from me. *(He's suddenly furious.)* I want you. Can't you understand that? I want you and it's choking me. Look at me: I don't know how to belong to my life. To be here. Not knowing where here is anymore. Am I here, Ginny? What you're looking at—is it me?

(After some moments)

GIN: I'm going into that plant with the rest of them. I'm going to work with glass. We're going to make it ours. But I'm a coward. If they come after us, I'll run too. But I won't live. Like this anymore.

DRAY: You want me to leave?

GIN: I want you to do something.

DRAY: I can't.

GIN: *(Calmly)* I love you. So. I'll leave you behind.

(End Scene Two)

Scene Three

(PACE and DALTON. PACE is dressed in her brother's clothes. DALTON holds out her dress to her. Something unsettling has happened between them, though we don't know what. PACE takes the dress, looks at it.)

DALTON: Pace. What was that? What just happened.

PACE: You tell me.

DALTON: That wasn't. No. That wasn't. Right.

PACE: *(Examining the dress)* You made it wet.

DALTON: I'm sorry. I didn't mean to.

(PACE throws the dress aside.)

PACE: Dalton Chance, when we're grown up, I want to stand here with you and not be afraid. I want to know it will be okay. Tonight. Tomorrow. That when it's time to work, I'll have work. That when I'm tired, I can rest. Just those things. Shouldn't they belong to us?

DALTON: What do you want from me?

PACE: I want you to watch me, to tell me I'm here.

DALTON: You're here. You don't need me to tell you.

PACE: Yes I do. So watch me. Whatever I do. Take a good look. Make some notes. Cause one day I might come back here to find out who I was—and then you're going to tell me.

DALTON: I don't. Damn it. I don't know what you mean.

PACE: Look, it's simple—

DALTON: *(Interrupts)* Stop it. Every time we meet, afterwards, it's like pieces of me. Keep falling off. It shouldn't be that way, Pace. Something's got to come clear. To make sense. I keep waiting. I can't do it anymore.

PACE: All right. Then tonight we'll run her.

DALTON: No. Not tonight.

PACE: Tonight.

DALTON: That's not what I'm waiting for. It's just a train.

PACE: Yeah. Well it's going somewhere. And it doesn't look back. Tonight, god damn it. You'll run it tonight.

DALTON: No. Not me. That was just a game.

PACE: We've been working on this for weeks. You can't back down. It's time. I can feel it. Everything's quiet. Everything's waiting. Listen? Here how quiet it is—

DALTON: *(Interrupts)* It's just talk, Pace. Just talk. This used to be fun. That's gone. You're gone. I don't know where but you're gone.

PACE: I could hurt you. *(She takes out her knife.)*

DALTON: I'm not afraid of your knife. You could cut me open but I'd still leave.

(PACE *jumps him and knocks him down. She sits on him.*)

PACE: What's the matter with you?

DALTON: You said you'd change me. You did, God damn it. Now change me back.

PACE: I can't.

DALTON: Yes you can.

PACE: How. Just tell me how.

DALTON: I don't know. How the hell am I to know? I didn't do it. You did it. You brought me here. You talked and talked. You put your hands inside my head. You kissed me without kissing me. Tonight. Finally tonight. But not like a girl should. You fucked me but I wasn't even inside you. It's ridiculous. This isn't how I want to be.

PACE: How do you want to be?

DALTON: Normal. Like any other kid. And satisfied. Like I used to be. Just satisfied. And now. Now I want everything. You did this to me.

PACE: Say it.

DALTON: No.

PACE: Say it.

DALTON: No.

PACE: I hate you, Pace Creagan.

DALTON: Yeah. I do!

(*Beat. He's quiet now.*)

DALTON: And there are times I've never been happier; I can't forgive you for that.

(PACE *touches* DALTON's *face gently, then gets off of him. She starts to leave.*)

DALTON: Where you going? Pace. Hey. Pace.

(She leaves.)

(End Scene Three)

Scene Four

(DALTON in his cell, still on his back. DRAY enters, quiet and bewildered. He carries a small pillow. At first, DALTON tries to ignore him.)

DALTON: I was just going to sleep.

DRAY: Yes. I know it's late.

DALTON: Why did you come?

DRAY: Isn't it natural a father would come?

DALTON: You've hardly left the house in months.

(DRAY holds out the pillow to DALTON.)

DRAY: I brought you your pillow.

(DALTON doesn't take it.)

DALTON: That's not my pillow.

DRAY: It's not?

DALTON: I haven't used it for years. The feathers are poking out of it. I used to wake up in the night and my face felt like it was full of nails.

(DRAY runs his hand over the pillow. He finds a feather and pulls it out.)

DRAY: Yeah. There's one. *(He finds another.)* Here's another.

(DRAY continues to gently comb and search the pillow and pull out a feather here and a feather there, sparingly, as the scene continues. DALTON watches this strangely tender exercise. DRAY looks at each feather he removes, then forgets it as he goes on to another. The feathers float unnoticed to the ground.)

DALTON: I don't sleep much in here anyway.

(*Watching* DRAY *pull the feathers*)

DALTON: So are you going to roast it after you pluck it?

DRAY: Not as bad as I though it'd be. Walking the street again.

DALTON: It's about time.

DRAY: Course I did have this pillow to hide my face in. You think anyone saw me?

DALTON: I hope not.

DRAY: There's something I want you to do for me.

DALTON: You think I killed her.

DRAY: I want you to touch me.

(DALTON *does not respond.*)

DRAY: Does the thought. Disgust you?

DALTON: You haven't let me. In a long time.

(DRAY *advances.* DALTON *is suddenly furious.*)

DALTON: Stop right there. Don't, god damn it! (*Beat*) You think you can come. In here. (*He rips the pillow out of* DRAY's *hands and throws it aside.*) After all this time with this fucking pillow and everything's going to be okay? Yeah. It disgusts me. You disgust me. Like a little fucking kid sitting in your corner week after week waiting for the world to stop. Well it did, Father. At least for me. No. I don't want to touch you. What difference could that make now? To me, you're just a noise in the corner. I won't even notice when you go.

(*They are quiet some moments.* DRAY *does not move to leave.*)

DALTON: Stay with me.

DRAY: I don't want to live. Like this.

DALTON: How?

DRAY: Unchanged. Your skin's warm. I can feel it from here. So close to me you smell of. Berries. I don't know. Gasoline. And somewhere behind it all something like, something like. I don't know. I don't— All my life I wanted to say something that mattered. *(Beat)* I don't know why I came.

DALTON: To bring me my pillow. *(Beat)* Go home.

(DRAY *sits.*)

DRAY: What happens when we die?

DALTON: How the hell should I know? You should be telling me that. I'm the one who's supposed to die. Christ, what's going on here? They're going to hang me. Do you understand? I told them I killed her.

DRAY: Did you kill her?

DALTON: I don't know.

DRAY: I think when we die, we just. Disappear. A few handfuls of nothing maybe. And that's it. What do you think?

(DALTON *sits down beside him, but not that close.* DALTON *shrugs.*)

DALTON: We just lie down and we don't get back up.

DRAY: Will it be terrible?

DALTON: Some people think there's a light. Some say it comes from above. I don't believe it. If there's anything at all, it'll come up from under the ground. Where we don't expect it. A light. A warm light and it'll cover us.

DRAY: What color is the light?

DALTON: Who knows.

DRAY: Red. I think it should be red.

DALTON: Yeah. Like the sun, when you look at it with your eyes closed. *(After some moments)* I'll touch you now. If you want.

DRAY: I'm going to close my eyes.

DALTON: Why?

DRAY: So no one will see us.

(DRAY *closes his eyes.* DALTON *awkwardly rests his head on his father's knee. It is a small gesture. They sit this way together some moments. Then* DALTON *lifts his head away again. After some moments of silence* DRAY *gets to his feet.*)

DALTON: Wait a minute. I want you to show me how to make a shadow on the wall. Any thing. I don't care what.

(DRAY *takes the pillow with him.*)

DRAY: It'll take too long.

DALTON: I got the time.

DRAY: (*Looking at the small bunch of feathers on the floor*) As though a bird had died here. (*He leaves.*)

DALTON: Wait a minute. Wait.

(DALTON *looks, surprised, at the floor around him.*)

(*The feathers stir as though a breeze had passed through them.*)

(*End Scene Four*)

Scene Five

(DRAY *meets* CHAS *as he leaves the cell. They stop and stare at each other. Elsewhere on stage, a feather falls on* DALTON, *though now* DALTON *does not seem to notice. A few more fall as the scene progresses.*)

CHAS: Never stops talking about you. Thinks you're a hell of a guy.

(DRAY *doesn't respond.*)

CHAS: Way a son should. Just like mine.

DRAY: He's dead.

CHAS: Looks pretty lively to me.

DRAY: *(Interrupting)* Yours. I mean.

(There is an awkward silence.)

CHAS: You're out of work. I've got this job.

DRAY: Your son was on the track team.

CHAS: I trained him. Out the old road to the cut-off in Eastwood.

DRAY: I've got to go.

CHAS: He says you do shadows.

DRAY: What of it?

CHAS: Hey. What's this? Your son never guessed it.

(CHAS imitates a plane doing a perilous landing. No sound. DRAY considers him carefully.)

DRAY: Baby elephant.

CHAS: Elephant? Like father like son. Wrong, but close. An aeroplane. Motor gone dead. Doing a dead-stick landing. In slow motion of course.

DRAY: Okay. This?

(DRAY acts out a camel. With full conviction. CHAS circles him, studying DRAY's every movement. DRAY seems to come alive in this charade, in a way we haven't witnessed before.)

CHAS: Nothing else but a camel, probably a dromedary.

(DRAY stands stunned.)

DRAY: Yeah.

CHAS: Not bad at all. Can you do a windmill?

DRAY: I got to go.

CHAS: Wait, wait, we just started. I could teach you. I'm teaching your son.

DRAY: Save it for your own. Good-bye. *(He doesn't move.)*

CHAS: I'm sort of practicing. For him. You know?

DRAY: You're pretty good.

CHAS: He was asking for that pillow.

DRAY: It's not his.

(DRAY leaves. We hear the sound of someone blowing air. As though they were blowing out matches, but more gently.)

(End Scene Five)

Scene Six

(PACE and DALTON sitting together, a few feet apart. PACE is blowing on a small feather. We hear the sound of her breath in the silence.)

(Then PACE blows the feather into the air, and keeps it above her head, blowing on it, just a little, each time it descends. She lets it land on her upturned face.)

(DALTON watches this. PACE sees him watching her. She gives him the feather. He tries to copy her. He does so badly. PACE just watches. And laughs. They are enjoying themselves.)

(Then DALTON "gets" how to do it. He blows the feather up and keeps it in the air. PACE watches him. Then he lets the feather float slowly down between them.)

(They are both quietly happy. Because they are no longer alone. Because they are watching each other just being alive.)

(End Scene Six)

Scene Seven

(CHAS *is sweeping up the feathers in the cell.* DALTON'*s back is turned.*)

CHAS: What do you expect? A hotel or something. There's holes in the roof. Sometimes they build a nest up there. It's the way of the world. They're moving you tomorrow. The trial'll start. It'll be the last of us. Empty cell. Might never get filled, then I'd have to find something else. Move to another jail. Might be no more criminals, not even a rich man who thinks he's a crab. Scuttlin' back and forth. Makes sweeping a devil's job. I can tell you. Still. (*He pokes the broom into* DALTON'*s turned back.*) You gonna tell them the truth this time? Only witness was you. Huh, huh? No explanation. No defense. Look, kid. If you talk, if you give them something to make them think you're crazy or sorry or scared, they might not hang you. If you don't talk, they will. Those are the facts.

(DALTON *doesn't respond.* CHAS *tutts at him.*)

CHAS: A nice-faced boy like you. I had a nice-faced boy. (*He keeps poking* DALTON *in the back.*) There was no substance to him. I could knock you down and sweep you up like you were nothing but a scrap of dust.

(*Suddenly* DALTON *turns and grabs the broom.*)

DALTON: Hey. Guess what this is?

(DALTON *slaps himself in the face. Then again. Then he starts to pull his own hair and hit himself, as though someone else is hitting him. He beats himself to the ground in an ugly, violent and awkward manner.* CHAS *watches. Slowly he backs away. They are silent.*)

CHAS: I've been good to you.

DALTON: Yeah. Brett was a nice boy. He used to hit himself. I saw him do it. Why was he like that? He was a fucking loon, that's why.

CHAS: Brett wasn't a loon. (*Beat*) Sometimes. Well. I hit him. In the mornings, right before he went to school. Just about the time he'd start on a bowl of cereal. And a lot of the time, she'd be there. Pace. Your Pace. But I'd hit him anyway. Brett liked her to see it. After I hit him, Brett would take Pace aside and ask her if she saw it. Of course she saw it. She was standing right beside him! But Brett wanted to make sure. Then one morning I'm just about to hit him when he says "Wait a minute, Dad. You've got a headache so you just sit back down and take it easy. I'll take care of it." So Brett hauls off and hits himself in the mouth. And I mean hard. His lip busts and starts bleeding. I'm so surprised that I sit back down and just stare at him. Next morning, the same thing. Brett stands in front of me and hits himself in the face. Twice. I don't say a thing. I just watch. Sometimes him doing it himself, instead of me, made us laugh. Together. The only time we did that. Laugh. (*Beat*) I knew Brett ran that train. It wasn't the first time. Maybe it was fate.

DALTON: It wasn't fate. It was a train. Five hundred and sixty tons of it.

CHAS: He was. My son. He was waiting. For me to give him something. I couldn't stand it; I didn't have anything to give him. A key to a cell, maybe. A broom to go with it. Is that what you give your child when he grows up? I didn't have anything to give him. So I hit him. I could give him that.

(DALTON *puts his hands in the feathers. He looks up.*)

DALTON: How do the birds get in? There's no hole in this roof.

CHAS: What do we do afterwards? I loved him. Years from now?

DALTON: What we wanted. It was to live. Just to live.

(CHAS begins sweeping again.)

CHAS: I got to finish up here. Word is there's gonna be trouble down at the Plate Glass factory. Might be some new guests to replace you any day now.

DALTON: About your son. I'm sorry.

CHAS: Ah. It seems so long ago now; it's all I think about. *(Beat)* Hey, last chance, kid. Guess what I am? *(He sweeps the broom a little wider, almost a figure eight motion, but without much effort.)*

DALTON: A giraffe. Grazing. The broom's your neck.

CHAS: No. Just an old man. Sweeping the floor of his cell.

(DALTON stops the broom with his hand.)

DALTON: Tell them I'm ready to talk.

CHAS: We're all asleep. It'll have to wait 'til morning. *(He leaves.)*

DALTON: Hey. I want to talk now. Open the door. Open up the fucking door! I got something to say.

(At first he shouts to CHAS, who is off-stage, then he speaks to himself and finally he is telling us, as though we were the jury, what happened.)

DALTON: *(Shouting)* Pace wanted to make the run that night. I wouldn't do it. I was afraid. No, I was angry.

(PACE appears. DALTON doesn't "see" her but sometimes senses she might be there.)

PACE: You messed all over my dress!

DALTON: But I didn't touch her! I was. Upside down. I was. God damn it—

PACE: You don't know what you were.

DALTON: I told her to run it alone.

PACE: You dared me.

DALTON: Pace never could say no to a dare. She stood on the tracks. She was covered in sweat. I stood below the trestle. She looked small up there, near a hundred feet above me. But until she started to run, I never thought she'd do it without me.

PACE: I had it made. Bastard. I needed you to watch—

DALTON: I could hear her footsteps. Fast, fast—

PACE: Because we can't watch ourselves. We can't remember ourselves. Not like we need to.

DALTON: Christ, I didn't know she could run like that! She was half way. She had it crossed. But then I.

PACE: Turned around. You just. Did it. (*She "disappears".*)

DALTON: Then I. Just did it. I turned. Around.

(DALTON *is propelled into the past moment. Now he can "see"* PACE. *But where he looks to see her, high up, we see nothing. The* PACE *that* DALTON *sees we cannot see, and the* PACE *we see, is not the* PACE *that* DALTON *sees. Elsewhere, we see* PACE *climbing up the trestle.* DALTON *shouts at the* PACE *we can't see.*)

DALTON: No! No way! I won't be your fucking witness! You're warped. That's what you are. Everybody says it. (*Beat*) Stop. You better stop!

PACE: (*She reappears, very high up on a what might be a piece of track. She calls to him.*) Dalton. Watch me. Hey! Watch me.

DALTON: No. Damn you.

(DALTON *turns around, so that his back is to both the* PACE *we can see, and the other* PACE *we cannot see.*)

PACE: Dalton. Turn around. Watch me.

DALTON: *(He is furious and torn as he covers his ears and shouts.)* God damn you, Pace Creagan!

(Now he is back in the present, and he speaks to us. PACE remains very still on the track.)

DALTON: But I wouldn't turn around. Pace must've slowed down. And lost her speed, when she was calling to me. Pace started to run back but she knew she'd never make it. And then she turned. Even from where I was at, I could see she was shaking her head. Back and forth, like she was saying: No. No. No. *(Beat)* She didn't want to die.

(PACE puts her arms over her head, like she is going to dive.)

DALTON: And then she did something funny. Pace couldn't even swim and there was no water in the creek, but she was going to dive.

PACE: Watch me. Dalton.

DALTON: And this time. I watched her.

(This time DALTON turns around, and for the first time looks at the PACE that we can also see. This time we all watch PACE.)

(PACE moves as if to dive, there is the tremendous, deafening roaring of a train that sounds almost like an explosion, different from the other train sounds we have heard. Then PACE is "gone" and we see nothing more of her. DALTON is "alone" and speaks quietly now.)

DALTON: Pace lay beside the trestle. She wasn't mashed up from the fall. Only the back of her head. I started to shout at her. Called her every name I could think of. Even a few she'd taught me herself. *(Beat)* And then. And then I did something. Something I can't. I don't know. It was. Maybe. It was. Unforgivable. I knelt beside her. Pace never let me kiss her, like that. So I did. And she didn't try to stop me. How could she? That's what I can't forget. She once said to me, Dalton, you can't take anything from me I don't want to give you. But then she opened her mouth. She was dead. But she opened her mouth. And I kissed her, the way I'd always wanted to. And she let me.<MI> *(Beat)* She let me. *(Beat)* I have to believe that.

(DALTON swipes the feathers aside. A moment later, we see CHAS again, who lets DALTON out of his jail cell. We hear the key unlocking the cell. We know DALTON is freed.)

(End Scene Seven)

Scene Eight

(GIN appears and watches DRAY. DRAY is still. GIN is holding a large piece of glass in her hands, which has a small break on one side.)

GIN: We've swept the place out. Most of the machinery's all right. Glass everywhere. Like hail. We scooped it up. By the bucketful. Three girls from my work are with me. About thirty others. From all over. We threw lots of this out. Thought I'd bring some home. We can use it in the back door. *(Calmly)* Put that away.

(Now we see that the shadow DRAY is making is a gun. And the gun is not a shadow.)

DRAY: I went to see Dalton. He said at night when he slept, his face was full of nails. All these years. And I didn't know. *(Beat)* Come here.

GIN: I've got to get back to the plant. Are you coming with me?

DRAY: Just come here.

(GIN stands by him.)

DRAY: Here.

(He gives her the gun. She just stands there with the gun, hanging at her side, ignoring it.)

GIN: Almost a shame to sweep up that glass. It was so bright in there. The sun through the windows, hitting the glass on the floor—

DRAY: *(He turns to* GIN *and lifts her hand so the gun is at his forehead.)* Ginny.

GIN: —like we were standing on a lake of ice that was turning to fire right under our feet.

DRAY: Change me.

*(*GIN *does not respond.)*

DRAY: Please. Please. Change me.

GIN: No. Not like that. *(She puts the gun down between them and moves away.)* Dray. Are you coming with me?

*(*DRAY *doesn't answer.* DRAY *makes a shadow on the wall. Then another)*

DRAY: What is it? A horse? A dog? I don't know anymore.

GIN: This is the last time I ask you: are you coming with me?

DRAY: *(Dropping his hands)* Shadows. Just fucking shadows.

*(*GIN *leaves.* DRAY *stands up, suddenly, knocking over his chair as he does so. He looks in the direction of* GIN's *exit and speaks softly.)*

DRAY: Yes. I am.

(End Scene Eight)

Scene Nine

(DALTON *is making shadows on the wall, as in the prologue.* PACE *appears behind him.* PACE *is dressed in her brother's clothes. She carries her dress. She lies it on the ground and spreads it out carefully.)*

PACE: That's a bird, stupid. A pigeon.

(DALTON *slowly turns around.)*

PACE: Like the kind that live under the trestle. Haven't you heard them? At dawn they make a racket. *(She's finished laying the dress out. She stands back.)* Lie down on it.

DALTON: Why?

PACE: Just do it. Or you'll be sorry. Last chance, Chance.

(DALTON *kneels down on the dress.)*

DALTON: What're you gonna do?

(PACE *jumps up onto a higher level and turns her back to* DALTON. *She is exhilarated.)*

PACE: Make something happen!

DALTON: Are you going to kick me? Are you mad at me?

PACE: Open your shirt.

DALTON: What?

PACE: Just shut up and do what I tell you. Open your shirt.

(DALTON *opens his shirt. Throughout their dialogue,* PACE *never touches herself.)*

PACE: Now. Touch me.

(DALTON *makes a movement towards her but she cuts him off.)*

PACE: No. Stay still. Right there. And do this. *(She puts her own hands near her chest, though she doesn't touch herself.)* Go on.

(DALTON copies her.)

PACE: Right. Now close your eyes. And touch me. It's simple.

(DALTON hesitates, then he closes his eyes and touches his own bare chest. PACE is very still, her arms at her side.)

PACE: Yes. There. You won't hurt me. *(Beat)* Go on.

(DALTON touches his nipples.)

PACE: That's right. You're touching me. I want you to touch me. *(She raises her arms in the air, still facing away from DALTON.)* It's going to happen. To both of us. Go on. Open your legs. *(Beat)* Do it.

(DALTON lies down, and opens his legs.)

PACE: Now touch me. There. Just touch me.

(DALTON touches himself.)

PACE: Can you feel me? I'm hard.

(DALTON moans. He turns over onto his stomach. PACE never looks at him, though she is just as involved as before.)

PACE: I want to be inside you.

DALTON: Pace.

PACE: Let me inside you.

DALTON: Go on. *(He makes a sharp intake of breath.)*

PACE: Does it hurt?

DALTON: Yeah.

PACE: Good. I can't stop.

(DALTON moans again, as though in both pain and pleasure.)

PACE: Now. Yes. Can you feel me?

DALTON: I'll make your dress wet—

PACE: Can you feel me?

DALTON: Yes.

PACE: Where? Tell me. Where can you feel me?

DALTON: Inside. Everywhere. Pace. *(Beat)* You're inside me.

(DALTON comes. They are quiet some moments.)

PACE: There. We're something else now. You see? *(Only now does she turn around.)* We're in another place.

(Both of them are quiet and still some moments. Then DALTON opens his eyes. He slowly stands up.)

(PACE moves towards the candle. PACE and DALTON look at one another.)

(PACE crouches over the candle. DALTON makes a slight movement, as though touching his mouth. PACE blows out the candle, at the same moment DALTON seems to do the same. We hear the sound of the candle going out. Then blackout)

END OF PLAY